For my mom and dad,
The origin of all love in my life.

—W.M.

This book is dedicated to all who feel overloaded and hurried—may you find peace and ease, and may that peace penetrate the entire world.

—J.B.

antley, MD

Wendy Millstine

five good minutes

100 morning practices to help you stay calm & focused all day long

New Harbinger Publications, Inc.

Publisher's Note

Distributed in Canada by Raincoast Books.

Copyright © 2005 by Jeffrey Brantley and Wendy Millstine
New Harbinger Publications, Inc.
5674 Shattuck Avenue
Oakland, CA 94609

Cover design by Amy Shoup
Text design by Amy Shoup and Michele Waters-Kermes
Acquired by Tesilya Hanauer
Edited by Brady Kahn

ISBN 1-57224-414-3 Paperback

New Harbinger Publications' Web site address: www.newharbinger.com

07   06   05

10 9 8 7 6 5 4 3 2 1

First printing

contents

1   wish yourself safety
2   five-fingered peace
3   in with the good . . .
4   instant ahhhh . . .
5   a silent retreat
6   drop it
7   laugh it off
8   go with the flow
    (of your breath)
9   sing to beat the blues
10 joyous rapture
11 loosen the grip
12 shower power
13 melt that frown
14 push all the right buttons
15 freedom from tension
16 push the "temporary"
    button

17 red light, blue light,
    feather light
18 rekindle the light
19 relax deeply

Peaceful Awareness and Connection   69

Growing Wiser and Kinder   175

71 name the pain
72 give grace
73 just when you thought you were alone
74 gorgeous on the inside
75 begin to heal your own deep pain
76 a shot of faith
77 bold, fearless, and powerful
78 face death with wisdom and compassion
79 mine your power
80 open the door to wisdom
81 feel your connection with all things
82 honor your commitments
83 the highway of life
84 be a mountain
85 one-way ticket to the moon
86 cultivate gratitude
87 fuel your optimism
88 the doctor is in
89 where the soul lives
90 live in this moment
91 dig yourself out of the pit
92 spell it out
93 retire the judges in your mind
94 creative juice squeeze
95 no more grumpy mornings
96 "no" is not a four-letter word
97 find life in death
98 infinite impossibilities
99 give yourself praise
100 open to the mystery of being human

introduction

Five minutes can seem so short—or so long. Life can be so busy, intense, rewarding, confusing, or overwhelming. Especially these days, it may seem—despite an abundance of things, as well as things to do—life can feel empty and unsatisfying.

Yet, in a breath, or a moment, everything can change.

This book is dedicated to helping you become more present, connect more fully, and enrich your life.

The concept is simple: Take the time, for just five minutes every morning, to be really present, to set a clear intention for yourself, and to throw yourself wholeheartedly into an easy-to-follow practice or activity.

Each practice or activity suggested in this book has the power to initiate change—change in your relationship to yourself, in your ideas about how you live and interact with others, in how you view your place in the world, or in your sense of meaning and purpose in life.

This book is for you if

- You would like to do more to enrich your life but are so busy and committed that you don't think you have time to add anything else.

- You just don't know what to do in order to feel happier or more satisfied.

- You often feel too tired or do not have the energy or strength to take on anything else, even something you want to do and know could help you.

- You are curious and willing to explore some different approaches to your inner and outer life and to the mystery of being human.

PART 1

the foundation

What Are Five Good Minutes?

Five minutes is clock time. The practices and activities in this book invite you to dwell in *the present moment*—which is always here and is timeless.

From the perspective of this book, five minutes of clock time begins to change into something much more powerful and interesting when you *are present* (attention is in the present moment, and not lost in thoughts of past or future), when you *set a clear intention* for your actions, and when you *act wholeheartedly*. When you apply attention, intention, and wholeheartedness to the exercises in this book, which are aimed at cultivating peace and relaxation, deepening awareness and connection to life; enhancing relationships, and developing kindness and wisdom, then your five minutes truly becomes *five good minutes.*

Why Five Minutes in the Morning?

The combination of attention, intention, and wholehearted-ness offers you a radically different way of approaching life. It suggests a method to awaken and to come off of "automatic pilot."

How do you usually begin your day?

Do the same thoughts, feelings, and worries fill your head, even as your eyes open in the morning? Do you handle them in the same ways? Does one day begin to feel too much like the previous one?

We all fall into habits of thinking, feeling, and acting. We seek distraction and relief and something better in our lives. Too many times, we don't know where to start. Yet, so much of what we seek is actually within us. The exercises in this book invite you to start, for five minutes. They invite you to be more playful, more experimental, more curious about your life. They offer a way to discovering something different—in yourself and about life.

It is best to do your five good minutes when you start your day. For most people, that is in the morning. (If you are on a different schedule, let the time you usually arise be the time for your practice.)

The morning is the best time to break away from old habits of thinking and feeling and to set a new direction for yourself and how you will be in your day. Any exercise in this book—done in the morning—has the power to impact greatly on your experience throughout the day, if you allow it!

Learning by Doing

As you experiment and practice with the hundred exercises in this book, you will learn to apply consciously your attention, intention, and wholeheartedness. You will see for yourself the power of being present and acting with intention while doing specifically guided exercises. Beyond the hundred exercises, you may even discover more ways to apply these same principles throughout your life.

To begin, all you need is some curiosity and the willingness to take the practices in this book seriously enough to try them.

You will learn to establish *presence*—an accepting and allowing awareness—by practicing mindful and kind attention to the simple sensations of your breath. Being present this way is the doorway to the timeless *now*. Mindful attention to the breath is not the only way to be more present, but it is a good way, and you always have your breath with you! Paying attention to the breath in a way that does not try to change, add, or subtract anything to the present moment has been practiced by human beings for thousands of years as a way to enter and remain in the present moment.

With presence established, dwelling more consciously in the present moment, you can set your *intention* for the activity or practice you have chosen.

Intention is potent. Nothing you do in this human life happens without some preexisting intention. Think of it. No movement, no action, happens without some thought or idea or intent beforehand. Many movements occur from intents that are unconscious or semiconscious, but if you pay close enough attention, you will observe the decision to act (or *react* if the decision is unconscious) before you act.

In your five good minutes, therefore, the second step is to set your intention. It might be, "May this meditation support peace and ease in my life." Or, it could be, "May this activity awaken humor and joy in me."

The remaining three to five minutes of your five good minutes are devoted to a specific exercise or activity. This book takes more than one approach. You don't have to like or even try all the exercises in this book. Feel free to work with the ones that speak to you. But you might also benefit from experimenting with things that do not initially appeal to you. Try to explore!

To review, here are the three easy steps to your five good minutes: establish presence through mindful breathing, set your intention, and then do the exercise or activity you have chosen wholeheartedly.

Many of the exercises in this book will invite you directly to breathe mindfully and to set your intention before moving to the remaining instructions. Others will not refer directly to *attention* and *intention* before giving the exercise instructions.

Even if it is not suggested directly, *it would be a good idea for you to breathe mindfully for a few breaths and to set an intention before you do any of the exercises in this book.*

To appreciate the power of attention and intention, you might even experiment by doing the same exercise *without* establishing attention and intention, then repeating it with them. See for yourself how powerful being present and setting intention really are for the experience of five good minutes.

Exercises and Activities

You will work with a variety of approaches in your five good minutes. They include the following:

Mindfulness is the awareness that arises as you pay attention on purpose with a friendly and accepting attitude to whatever is present. Being mindful means being present consciously. Being mindful is at the heart of your five good minutes. Mindfulness of your breath is how you establish presence. The exercises in this book aim to help you become more mindful in different places and in different ways in your daily life.

Meditation is an activity of directing your attention, so you will become more aware and more understanding and wise.

Meditation is about much more than simple relaxation. Some meditation methods emphasize narrowing your attention to a single object or a quality. Other meditation practices focus upon developing a clearer and deeper awareness of what is happening. The meditation practices in this book include both approaches. They promote calm attention and awareness for feeling more ease and peace, for greater understanding, and for the development of desirable qualities, such as kindness, compassion, and joy.

Imagery is the thought process that involves and uses the senses: vision, audition, smell, taste, and the senses of movement and position. You use your imagination to facilitate communication between perception, emotion, and bodily change. It is one of the world's oldest healing resources.

Acting wholeheartedly is central to all the activities. There are suggestions here for doing everyday things just a little differently—being more present and mindful, connecting more completely with what you do in the present moment, then singing, laughing, dancing, eating, listening—in short, participating in a whole array of experiences wholeheartedly. See for yourself the difference being present can make!

What Happens Next?

When you do your five good minutes, it is important to expect nothing more. Just be as present as possible in the five minutes and pay attention throughout the rest of the day. Notice how the exercise you do can echo and inform your experience.

Doing just one of these exercises with presence and intention has the power to change how you feel and relate to your life. Yet don't be discouraged if it seems nothing is different. You can also think of the five good minutes as planting a seed. It can take some time for a seed to grow. Again, a good idea is to just do it and to expect nothing. You never know when one of these practices will be a doorway for you, or a new beginning, or even a lifeline. Just keep alert to what does happen.

And, of course, you can experiment with more than five minutes in any of the exercises.

And you can do your five good minutes more than once each day.

And you can carry your favorite five good minutes practice further and deeper by doing them more often, by reading and learning more about any subject that the practice suggests, and by associating with others who enjoy similar activities.

In other words, your five good minutes in the morning might just change your life.

Your Gateway to the Present Moment

"Breathe mindfully for about a minute."

You will see this phrase at the beginning of many of the exercises in this book.

Why?

To be mindful means to connect with experience unfolding in the present moment—by paying deep and nonjudging attention. Practicing mindfulness promotes *presence*—the capacity to sense the immediacy of experience in each moment.

Any action you do, indeed, your involvement in any activity (including your five good minutes), is enormously amplified by the extent you are present with awareness.

Despite a desire to be more present for life, however, everyone has habits of inattention, distraction, and absence. These habits separate you from the richness in life's moments and from people with whom you wish a closer and more lasting connection.

Learning to practice mindful breathing, as you will in this book, can help you overcome habits of inattention and be more present for yourself and for life. By practicing even one minute of mindful breathing before setting an intention and doing the rest of your five good minutes, you will be establishing yourself more fully in the present moment. This will add more power to the exercise you are doing.

To breathe mindfully means to become a kind observer of your own breath sensations as they move in and out of your body. As you become an increasingly sensitive observer, you will begin to notice different qualities in each breath, in or out, and the space between the breaths as well.

Mindful breathing (also known as *awareness of breathing,* or *mindfulness of breathing*) is one of the most ancient and profound meditation practices available to human beings. Mindful breathing can be done by anyone, regardless of faith. Whoever you are, paying attention on purpose and nonjudgmentally to the sensations of your breath is an effective way to dwell in the present moment and to avoid being lost in the wanderings of your own mind.

In addition to doing the meditation practices in this book, you may want to explore longer periods of meditation using the instructions below for mindful breathing.

Instructions for Mindful Breathing

The following instructions are one way to practice mindful breathing. Some of the exercises in this book will elaborate further on mindful breathing. You may also be aware of other variations on these instructions.

Whatever the exact wording may be, mindful breathing is essentially about your willingness to reside in the present moment with your kind and nonjudging attention focused primarily on the sensations of your breath. From that primary focus, your relationship to all other experience shifts.

Please remember also that you can do mindful breathing in any position—sitting, lying down, or standing—and even while moving.

Now, let the following instructions guide you as you practice mindful breathing here and later in this book.

① Take a comfortable position, one that supports you in being awake.

② Turn your attention on purpose to the direct physical sensations happening as you breathe. You may wish to close your eyes if it helps you focus attention on your breath sensations.

③ Find a place in your body, the tip of your nose, or your abdomen, for example, where you can actually feel the breath moving in and out.

④ Rest your attention there, where you can feel your breath most easily.

⑤   It is not necessary to control your breath in any way in this meditation. Simply allow your body to breath as it does, and pay attention as best you can to the direct sensations of the moving breath.

⑥   As you direct kind attention to your breath sensations, set down all of your burdens—inner and outer ones—for the time of this meditation. It is not necessary to make anything happen nor to become anything other than who you are in this moment.

⑦   When you notice that your attention has wandered off of the breath sensations, notice where it went, and gently but firmly bring your attention back. You have not done anything wrong when this happens. The mind will move off of the breath countless times. Each time, practice kindness and patience with yourself, notice where your mind went, and bring attention back to the breath.

⑧   Let the meditation support you. Rest attention on the changing patterns of sensation and breath. Move your attention closer, noticing the quality of each new breath as accurately and as continuously as possible. Stay present to the entire breath cycle: in, pause, out, pause, in, and so on. Notice how each breath has its own character.

⑨   End your meditation by shifting your focus off of the breath sensations, opening your eyes, and moving gently.

Set Your Intention

Setting an intention is a way of pointing yourself in a direction, toward an important value or goal. It is a way to identify a quality you wish to nurture in your life.

Setting intention can be done skillfully or unskillfully.

It is not so skillful or effective to be rigid or attached to an ideal about your intention. For example, if your intention is to foster ease and self-acceptance, don't expect to become 100 percent relaxed or self-accepting after just five minutes! Be careful that you don't make your intention, no matter how wonderful or positive, something else on your to-do list or something you must achieve at all costs! Recognize the trap of judging yourself harshly or doubting your intention if things don't change right away. Don't fall into that trap of judgment and doubt.

A skillful intention is more like a friendly guide. Acknowledge from the beginning that important changes take time. You, like everyone else, must make the effort to return repeatedly to the goal you seek.

Your intention, to become more self-accepting, for example, is better thought of as a direction you have selected for yourself. The practice you choose is a way to enter on a path moving in that direction. Results aren't always so obvious. Many conditions and factors are at work as you move along your path. What is important is that you keep moving in the right direction. Being friendly with yourself as you travel the path is vital. Being patient with yourself as you move toward your goal is crucial.

You can think of your intention as a clear and strong statement of an important value, quality, or goal you have selected for yourself. Through the single act of making the statement, you have opened the door for a profound shift in your life.

Act Wholeheartedly

To act wholeheartedly means to do something with all of your attention and energy. Establishing presence and acting from clear intention will support you in embracing what you do wholeheartedly. In your five good minutes, after establishing presence and stating an intention, you are invited to embrace the practice you have selected wholeheartedly.

You may have to experiment a bit with being whole-hearted. Much of what we do in life is done without full attention, or without real commitment to the activity or process, for a variety of reasons. So, as you begin to try out the exercises in this book, give yourself some room to grow. At first, you may not feel wholehearted about every one of the exercises. Some may even be a turnoff.

To get the most of your five good minutes, start with activities that resonate with you, or that seem especially interesting, or are perfect for something happening in your life right now. As you work with the various practices over time, notice how different ones fit in the different corners and phases of your life.

When you have selected practices that seem to fit, nurture a willingness to experiment with them, without expecting too much at first. Even if you feel awkward, silly, or embarrassed, just acknowledge how you feel and then keep on with the practice.

You may find it easier to be wholehearted if you let go of trying to change anything or make anything happen as you do the exercises. This is a paradox that is true of many of the practices in this book. In the realm of transformation and growth, the more you reach for something, the farther away it can seem.

So let go of any attachment to outcome and just dive right in! Instead of vigilantly monitoring what is happening, looking for changes, when dancing, or laughing, or whatever you are practicing, just let go of judgment and do it. That way, you are truly acting wholeheartedly and, paradoxically, are maximizing your chances for change and growth.

PART 2

the practices

establishing ease
& inner relaxation

1

wish yourself safety

The feeling of safety is priceless and often elusive. Even the possibility of safety may at times seem unreachable.

There is profound power in the simple gesture of wishing safety for yourself. As a meditation, this practice is done in the same spirit of a parent holding a frightened child and lovingly whispering soothing words.

①   Breathe mindfully for about a minute.

② Set your intention. For example, "May this practice support a deeper peace and ease in me."

③ Relax, let your eyes close, and imagine a picture of yourself.

④ Bring compassionate attention to yourself, as a parent would to a child.

⑤ For the next few minutes, imagine speaking directly to yourself, whispering a phrase like "May I be safe from all harm," or, "May I be protected from all inner and outer harm." Wish yourself safety with the same spirit you would wish a dear friend a safe trip.

⑥ End by opening your eyes and moving gently. ☀

2

five-fingered peace

With a little practice, in just five minutes you can induce a highly effective relaxation technique using just your hand. Follow the steps below to guide yourself to a centered, focused state of awareness.

① Touching your thumb to your index finger, travel back to a time when you felt a healthy exhaustion after exerting yourself physically, such as cleaning house, mowing the lawn, or biking.

②　Touching your thumb to your middle finger, travel back in time to a loving exchange with someone special, such as a devoted love letter, a tantalizing sexual experience, or a heart-expansive conversation.

③　Touching your thumb to your ring finger, try to recollect the most caring gesture you have ever received. Take this opportunity to truly accept this gift.

④　Touching your thumb to your little finger, travel back to the most magnificent place that you've seen or dreamed about. Take this moment to absorb all the beauty that surrounds you.

This five-finger relaxation is your ticket to building inner strength, harmony, and a sense of ease. ✺

3

in with the good . . .

When you take the time to get in tune with your breathing, you begin to harness the vital life skills for returning to your calm, inner self. Sitting or lying down, place your hand on your abdomen and inhale and exhale, deeply and slowly. Visualize a meadow with a small creek running through it. You are wading in a babbling brook, and you can hear the wind and the birds overhead. The current tugs gently at your ankles. Recognize the rhythm of your breathing. As you inhale, say the word "warm" aloud. Imagine the warmth of the sun and water around your body. As you exhale, say the word "heavy" to yourself. Allow yourself to reach a comfortable and soothing place from within. Conscious breathing is a technique that can restore calmness to your day easily, in less than five minutes.

4

instant ahhhh . . .

When you are triggered by stress and anger, you need a way to induce relaxation instantly. You need a cue, like the command "Relax," in order to reduce your anxiety as quickly as possible. Get comfortable in a seated position. Take a deep breath and hold it for an extra moment. When you release this breath, focus on blowing your worries far away. Let go of any excess tension still residing in your body. Continue to breathe in and out, deeply and rhythmically, saying to yourself silently, "Breathe in" on the inhale and "Relax" on the exhale. Follow this repetition for five minutes:

Breath in . . . relax . . .

Breath out . . . relax . . .

Breath in . . . relax . . .

Breath out . . . relax . . .

Breath in . . . relax . . .

Breath out . . . relax . . .

With each breath, peace and calm comes in, and tension and stress move out. ☀

5

a silent retreat

Take five minutes to quiet your mind. Turn off the radio. Ask the kids to give you a few precious moments without a sound. In the silence, you can notice your breathing, your anxiety, your urgency. In the silence, you can stretch your mind to a place of calmness, less stress, no rush to be anywhere but right where you are. A moment in silence can set the tone for the rest of your busy day. With your eyes open or closed, the calming powers of silence can cloak you through any stressful situation. Keep this center of calmness and stillness with you where ever you go. The restorative power of silent solitude can be used to give you a sense of ease. ✺

6

drop it

Self-hypnosis is a simple skill that allows you to quickly reach a peaceful place. Dangle a pencil a few inches above a table. Let your eyes gently focus on the tip of the pencil. When you've reached a deeply relaxed state of mind, the pencil will drop. The sound of the pencil hitting the table will alert you to summon a healing, five-minute meditative trance. Begin your self-hypnosis by saying to yourself, "I am drifting off into a deep, deep, tranquil space . . . I am beginning to feel sleepy and drowsy, drowsy and sleepy . . . My eyes are heavy and my body is relaxed and letting go . . . I am free of all unnecessary thoughts and feelings . . . I am floating, drifting, drifting and floating, into a place of total relaxation." If your pencil has not dropped by this time, release it now, and enjoy the next few minutes of a serene hypnosis. ❁

7

laugh it off

The alarm has just gone off, and the urge to go back to sleep is insistent. There is nothing funny about waking up for work; you're likely thinking about why you didn't get enough sleep, or who stole all the covers, or how *someone's* snoring kept you up half the night. What could possibly be funny about this awful hour in the morning? What person in their right mind wakes up laughing, asks your tired, grumpy self.

①　Lying on your back, eyes closed, think back on a ridiculous thing you (or someone you know) did that now makes an outrageously hilarious story.

②　Remember a time you laughed really hard. Who were you with? What happened to make you laugh?

See if you can coax a chuckle out of your calamities. Learn to laugh at yourself more often. Lighten up, so laughter can spill forth from your everyday routine. ✳

8

go with the flow (of your breath)

The busyness and frantic pace of modern life can seem unending, overwhelming, and inescapable. In truth, relief is only a mindful breath away.

You can connect with a deep sense of inner calm and spaciousness by practicing mindful breathing. This is the same *mindful breathing* you have already done in this book. Here you can deepen what you know.

① Breathe mindfully for about a minute.

② Set your intention. For example, "May this practice give rise to deep peace within me."

③ Sit quietly, and set all your burdens down—the inner ones and the outer ones.

④ You don't have to do anything else. You don't have to make anything happen. Just allow yourself to relax, soften, and observe, following the breath sensations, and the movement of your attention between breath and other things.

⑤ End by opening your eyes and moving gently. ☀

9

sing to beat the blues

Most of us think that we can't sing or hold a note. But the truth is that we're too embarrassed. Singing, as a form of healing and releasing of negative feelings, dates back many centuries and is a tradition shared by every culture known to humankind. Take this time to find a song that you know you would enjoy singing along to. Give yourself permission to sing at the top of your lungs. Experience the wind filling your vocal cords. Notice the ebb and flow of your stomach muscles. Music and song can make you feel giddy, bubbly, euphoric, and joyful. Observe the sensations and feelings that arise while you are singing. Let your song be a pleasant reminder through your daily routine that singing can lift your spirit, alter a crummy day, or put an extra skip in your step.

10

joyous rapture

Everyone has experienced moments of joy. If joy were a river, we would do everything we could to bathe in it every day. Take five minutes to make a list of the experiences and events that bring you joy, such as, fishing, reading, jogging, sewing, spending time with your child, making love, gardening, playing an instrument, singing, doing something nice for someone less fortunate, receiving flowers, doing arts and crafts, surprising a loved one with a gift, winning an award, reaching a goal, talking with a close friend, riding your bicycle, walking through a park, sitting at the beach, eating a ripe peach, having a good belly laugh, feeling the sun on your face, taking an afternoon nap, or playing with your pet. The list goes on and on, much like a river. When you take note of the little joys in your life, you open yourself to more happiness. ✸

11

loosen the grip

Do you ever want to let go of something—an unpleasant feeling, a memory, or a worry? Perhaps all you really need is to remember how it feels to let go.

The following practice is a way of understanding the physicality and feeling of letting go. You can learn to link this physical experience of recognition and release with tightness around thoughts or feelings.

① Breathe mindfully for about a minute.

② Set your intention. For example, "May this practice empower me to recognize patterns of holding and tightening in myself and to release them."

③ Breathe mindfully for a few breaths. Then make a fist with one hand.

④ Squeeze the fist hard. Then gently but quickly release it. Repeat, focusing on the sensations of contracting and releasing.

⑤ Notice how the feelings extend through your body and inner life.

⑥ Whenever you have a painful feeling or emotion, look mindfully for a feeling of contraction or holding in your body. Work with the physical feeling directly. Explore the effect that easing the physical tightness has on the painful feeling. ✺

12

shower power

The healing and therapeutic benefits of a five-minute morning shower are not to be underrated. Spoil yourself with a warm, soothing shower. It's good for your body and your mind, releasing tension, washing away the cobwebs of sleep, and getting you off on a fresh foot. While you're in the shower, pay attention to the heat of the water on your body. Where does your body seem to crave it the most? Your neck, back, feet? Close your eyes and let it cascade over your head. Imagine washing away your sleepiness and reenergizing your body for the rest of the day. Be mindful of how invigorated you feel after a shower. The healing properties of water can revive your body, increase your circulation, reduce your aches and pains, and recharge you.

13

melt that frown

Don't let a burdensome frown shadow your whole day. Find things to smile about. Smile at the most unexpected times, and see if it doesn't change your attitude in an uplifting way. Take five minutes to keep a smile on your face in the morning:

- in the shower

- taking out the garbage

- washing the dishes

When you feel your face muscles relax, coax a smile back on. Imagine that you are stimulating vital facial muscles that you will need for the rest of your life. This exercise will greet you throughout your whole day. It will find you unexpectedly while you wash your face, pick up your dry cleaning, or stop at the market.

Look for a smile in the most absurd places, such as, your pathetic sock drawer, the weird way the sun casts a bizarre shadow on the carpet in the shape of a naked person, the curious look on your cat or dog's face.

If you find yourself caught in a mind-numbing daze, smile while you work. By shifting your thoughts in a positive way, you can lift your mood. It's hard to be bored, angry, or sad with a smile on your face. Let your mood take its lead from your smile. Who says your daily routine and chores have to be serious? ☀

14

push all the right buttons

Stress is a part of life. Wouldn't you love to have a button you could push to turn off stress and an equally useful button to turn on relaxation? Well, you can, by simply acknowledging the triggers that set you off and imagining the button that calms you down. You can retrain yourself to push the *right* buttons that allow you to relax and feel at ease.

① Recall a stressful time in your week. Notice your feelings and thoughts and how your body reacted.

② Now imagine a knob—much like the one on your stereo—that turns down the volume of stressful thoughts. When you feel yourself reacting to troubling thoughts, turn the volume down.

③ To the right of the stress knob is a button for instant calmness where peaceful and reassuring thoughts can be heard. Press the button.

Create a mantra or a key phrase that you can say to yourself, such as, "I have everything that I need to deal with this situation." By learning how to adjust the volume on stress, you instantly deescalate the strain and anxiety that may arise in your day. When you employ your visual relaxation button, you remind yourself that no situation is insurmountable. ☀

15

freedom from tension

Our bodies are a breeding ground for tension. We might store up tension for weeks before we know it's there. Headaches, backaches, and other physical pains are the voices of our bodies crying out for attention. Acknowledge and release your tension using a body scan technique.

① Lying down, take five minutes to scan where tension lives in your body.

② Start at the top of your head and move along down your neck, back, arms, and legs, taking note of the areas where you store your stress.

③ Once you have identified those areas, follow a simple guided imagery of becoming a free-floating cloud. High above the skyline, you are impervious to all negative thoughts and tension. In your free-floating bliss, all muscles and pains are released and set free.

Carry this imagery with you for any occasion to bring a sense of tranquillity to your week. ✳

16

push the "temporary" button

During times of stress, loneliness, anger, or depression, it's important to know that everything is in a constant state of change, that nothing stays the same. What you are feeling now will soon pass. This exercise will help you to locate the "temporary" button when you need it the most.

① Reflect on a time when you felt like the sadness would never go away. When you are in the throes of a burdensome emotion, it's not easy to imagine it passing over very quickly.

②   Take five minutes to visualize a button that you can press to remind you of the impermanence of the moment.

③   Recall a time when the difficult situation eventually eased up.

Keep your temporary button on you at all times. When stress unleashes, tell yourself, "This will pass, as do all unbearable moments in life. This won't last forever, and soon I will be back on a fresh, new path." ✽

17

red light, blue light, feather light

Take the next several minutes to visualize your whole body infused with red and blue lights. The red lights represent tension, and the blue lights represent relaxation. You can adjust the lights from brighter to dimmer, from bigger to smaller. Observe the areas in your body where the lights are red. Now imagine the red lights are just feathers. Pick them up. See yourself opening a window and tossing out your tensions into the wind. Go ahead and dump them all. Watch them flutter and move farther and farther away. As they disappear from your sight, so will they disappear from your awareness. Be aware of the sensation of all the blue lights of calmness circulating throughout your body. Relax further by visualizing all the blue lights becoming deeper and darker shades. Soon all your tension will be replaced by tranquillity. ✺

18

rekindle the light

Each of us has a radiant inner fire of beauty, strength, and wisdom. The problem is we forget how to keep the embers glowing. In the dampness of boredom or just forgetfulness, we burn out and turn off. We may not notice at first, but over time our light of hope gets extinguished by neglect. Use the following candle meditation as a guide to rekindle your inner light.

① Start by lighting a candle by your bedside or at your table to accompany you in your morning routine.

② Stare into the flickering flame and imagine the same flame igniting in the center of your soul.

③ Imagine this fire as the source of your hope, your dreams, your blessings, and your happiness.

④ Feed the flame by offering it protection, compassion, and understanding.

⑤ Remember to acknowledge your inner light daily.

19

relax deeply

How often do you wish you could calm down or just relax? Everyone has a built-in capacity for deep relaxation, but they may not appreciate or know how to access it. This practice will teach you a way to connect with your own ability for deep inner relaxation.

① Breathe mindfully for about a minute.

② Set your intention. For example, "May this practice of deep relaxation bring me health and ease."

③ Focus mindfully on the sensations of your breath, in and out.

④ Imagine that you are inhaling calm and peace. With each out-breath, exhale any unnecessary tension in your body.

⑤ Breathe this way for a few more minutes. Let the actual flow of your breath support you, bringing in peace and carrying out tension.

⑥ End by opening your eyes and moving gently. ✿

peaceful awareness
& connection

20

the life inside of you

Despite its richness, the inner life—with its thoughts, feelings, and sensations—often goes unnoticed. Yet these same thoughts, feelings, and sensations drive and shape much of your experience, unconsciously, moment by moment.

To make your thoughts, feelings, and sensations more conscious in the present moment is to become empowered. The following meditation practice offers you a means of recognizing and discerning more clearly the events and flow of your inner life.

1. Breathe mindfully for about a minute.

2. Set your intention. For example, "May this practice of inner awareness bring me health and wisdom."

3. Continue mindful breathing.

4. When you notice your attention leaving your breath, going to thoughts or to sounds, for instance, name where it went, quietly to yourself.

5. For the next few minutes simply sit, notice, and name the places in your inner world where your attention goes.

6. End by opening your eyes and moving gently. ✺

21

river of thoughts

Some days our minds are cluttered with unwanted thoughts. Endless, negative preoccupations and worries steal away our precious energy and leave us drained at the end of the day. Take this moment to reflect on your anxiety-provoking thoughts. Now imagine that you are writing them down on little pieces of paper. Once you have a sufficient stack, in your mind take a walk to the nearest river. At the river's edge, toss out your harassing thoughts, one by one, saying good-bye to each one. Watch the current carry your worries, like delicate leaves, down the river. Notice each nagging thought drift away and out of sight. Use this river to dump out any unwanted anxiety. Return to it whenever you need to empty your mind. ✹

22

the perfect escape

During times of fear and panic, it can be helpful to conjure up a special place that you know will interrupt your train of thought. Take a few minutes to rehearse a visualization of a place that you can evoke effortlessly and readily at any time. Your special place could be the following:

- an exciting cruise to an exotic country

- a day at the beach, waves splashing on the shore

- an exhilarating sexual fantasy

- a daydream that you are canoeing down a gentle stream with colorful fish gliding alongside you.

Imagine that you are having the time of your life—laughing, smiling, enjoying the company of loved ones, eating good food, and feeling relaxed. You are free to return to this special place whenever you need to instill a calming sense of well-being. ✳

23

connect with sound

Close attention to sounds—listening deeply—can awaken a sense of connection to life and access to an experience of vast interior spaciousness.

This practice is a way to explore your connection to life through sounds. Try it indoors and outdoors.

①   Breathe mindfully for about a minute.

②   Set your intention. For example, "May deep listening reveal richness and awe in my life."

③ Breathe mindfully for a few more breaths.

④ Shift attention from your breath to the sounds around you, paying attention to them and allowing them, without judgment or preference, to be there.

⑤ Listen to all that reveals itself: soft, loud, pleasing, annoying, even to the space between the sounds. Welcome each sound with deep attention.

Listen for a few more minutes. End by opening your eyes and moving gently. ✺

24

soften your mind

Anger can dominate thought processing. Anger has many triggers that can sabotage a perfectly good day. It is like a poisonous injection of fury that can be an obstacle to getting off on the right foot. This exercise is a guided meditation whereby you imagine ways to soften your mind and release your volatile side.

    ①   Recall a time when you felt particularly distressed or frustrated, which led you to feel angry.

②   Sitting or lying down, eyes closed, shoulders relaxed, become aware of your breathing.

③   As you inhale, take in enough air to fill your lungs with serenity. On the exhale, empty your lungs of your negativity and anger.

④   On the next big inhale, expand your chest cavity to receive the vitality of joy and goodness. On the next big exhale, release the darkness of anger that may still be clinging to you.

Use this breathing exercise whenever you feel upset. It will lift your mood and free you from angry thoughts. ☀

25

life below the neck

Do you live mostly above your neck? That is, in your head? Or do you live a few feet from your body, always moving your focus ahead of it? Or a few days or weeks distant from your body, with attention directed to the past or to the future?

The following is a simple mindfulness practice to help you become more aware and connected with your body.

① Breathe mindfully for about a minute.

② Set your intention. For example, "May mindful attention to my body bring me greater ease and health."

③ Sit or lie down comfortably, and allow your eyes to close.

④ Begin with mindful breathing, then widen your focus to include all sensations arising and changing in your body. Allow yourself to feel each sensation as it happens.

⑤ Explore different regions or areas: a foot, your back, or your face, for example. Without judgment, just allow and feel any sensations.

⑥ End by opening your eyes and moving gently.

26

nature's gift to you

Nature is bountiful and plentiful, and yet we often forget to take notice of nature's simple gifts of joy and serenity. Take five minutes, and like the old saying goes ...

- Stop and smell the flowers.

- Notice the flight of a bumblebee.

- Listen to the rustle of the wind through the trees.

- Take in the majestic beauty of a mountain range.

- Smell the salty scent of the sea air.

Keep a mindful awareness and appreciation of all the beauty that surrounds each moment. When you take this time to open your senses to the pleasures of what is just outside your door, you open your mind and body to nature's restorative power to soothe and heal you. ✱

27

license to do nothing

We live in a world that demands our constant attention. Things to do. Places to go. People to see. Errands to run. Kids to pick up. It is a never-ending list of productivity with hardly a millisecond to just relax. You now have an official pass-and-collect-five-minutes-to-do-absolutely-nothing ticket. Take the next entire five minutes and *do nothing!*

- Turn off the phone and ask family or roommates to not disturb you.

- Let your mind wander.

- Shrug off your to-do list or any distractions.

- Just imagine every nagging worry rolling off your shoulders and flushing down the toilet. This may require that you flush several times over, just to make sure you properly discard every pesky reason why you *should* be doing this or *should* be doing that.

That's right, lie down, kick back, relax, meditate on the ceiling, stare at your bookshelf, let yourself just be present in this suspended, timeless, empty moment. It's all yours. ✸

28

take a musical break

Take five minutes in the morning and listen to a violin concerto or a piano piece by Chopin. If you prefer jazz, a piece from Miles Davis's *Kind of Blue* or John Coltrane's *My Favorite Things* may be a nice alternative. Make sure that the music isn't pumping hard rock, but something more meditative. If you want something more energetic, consider Dvorak's Symphony no. 9, *From the New World*.

Once you have selected the appropriate song, let the music transport your mind to another place and time. Drift off to the last camping trip or vacation you took. Remember a time when you went to a see a live orchestra play for the first time.

Music has a soothing effect on the nerves. Music has the power to stir up warm memories, to make you smile inside, and to calm your inner spirit. ❁

29

really taste your food

Where is your attention when you eat? Do you ever see an empty plate before you and wonder who ate the food? Do you ever eat from boredom or worry, instead of hunger?

This practice invites you to become more mindful as you eat. By paying mindful attention as you eat, and connecting to the unfolding experience, including your inner life, you can find more pleasure and the possibility for a healthier life.

① When you sit down to eat breakfast, breathe mindfully for at least a few breaths.

② Set your intention. For example, "May eating mindfully make me healthier."

③ As you begin to eat, with the very first bite, pour all of your attention into the process. Notice how the food looks, smells, tastes, for each bite. Notice sensations of chewing and swallowing.

④ Let go of all other thoughts, plans, reading, television, computers, music—all of it.

⑤ For the next few bites, just pay attention to your experience of eating, including your inner life, allowing it to unfold without interference.

⑥ Enjoy! Discover! Become healthier!

30

write to clear your mind

Keeping a journal can be a healthy outlet for letting go of the tedious clutter of thoughts and freeing yourself to be more forgiving, compassionate, and less burdened by all the pressures in life. Take a little time to write down your thoughts in the morning. This exercise will help you clear out the disorder and confusion in your mind and free up your creative space. To help you get started, consider the following questions as suggestions for getting you off on the right foot.

- Write whatever comes to mind.

- Don't worry about punctuation, grammar, or spelling.

- Simply be in the moment with your random thoughts and feelings.

- What are you thinking, feeling, dreaming, imagining, or hoping for?

Writing enables you to access parts of your deeper self. When you transcribe your thoughts and feelings on paper, you are opening a gateway in your psyche for healing. ❁

31

connect deeply with something pleasant

Habits of inattention and distraction are so strong that they can actually interfere with your capacity to enjoy pleasant moments. This practice invites you to apply mindfulness and to enjoy deeply the benefits of full attention to pleasant experience.

①   First, prepare for a pleasant activity. For example, choose a favorite piece of music, select a favorite food, or go to a favorite place.

②   Then, breathe mindfully for about a minute.

③   Set your intention. For example, "May this practice help me connect more fully with joy and beauty in my life."

④   Begin your activity. Pay attention to all that occurs, without judgments or expectations.

⑤   Let go of any thoughts or stories as they arise, and simply stay with your experience. Take note of any aspects of the experience that call to you.

⑥   Open yourself to sights, sounds, smells, tastes, and sensations in the experience, as they arise.

⑦   Notice the feeling of joy or pleasantness itself and where that feeling is in your body.

⑧   When the experience ends, let it go. Breathe mindfully for a few breaths, and feel complete. ✻

32

your first sip of tea

Make yourself a cup of your favorite tea (or a beverage of your choice) in your favorite cup. Place the mug with the loose tea or teabag at your place at the table. As you pour water into the cup, pay attention to the way your body moves, the weight of the kettle, and the sound and look of the water. Be mindful of every movement as you replace the kettle on the stove and sit at the table in front of the teacup. Wrap your hands around the cup and breathe the steam in, paying attention to how it feels on your face, the smell of the tea, and the warmth of the cup in your hands. Look at the tea and notice how it moves or swirls as you lift the cup. Be mindful of its color. When you sip the tea, pay close attention to how it feels on your tongue, the complexity of the taste, and the movement of your tongue and lips. It should take you five minutes to swallow your first sip of tea. ❁

33

get grounded

As a child, you probably played in sandboxes. Whether you were aware of it or not, you learned that getting your hands in the dirt was a way to help yourself feel grounded. Take five minutes to play in the dirt. Your backyard, a flower box, or even a houseplant will do. Contemplate the following questions:

- Is the soil wet, dry, crumbly, or hard?

- What is it about dirt that you do or don't like?

- What are some of the things the soil produces that you cannot live without?

When you connect with nature, you connect to all living things. By sifting your hands through some soil, you can open yourself to the healing and grounding qualities of nature. ✺

34

the extraordinary in the ordinary

Our everyday routines can get drab. If you watch enough television, it can appear as though everyone is having the time of their lives, a lifetime full of one adventure after another. This exercise is about finding the miraculous in daily life, searching for the unique in the mundane, or imagining the unimaginable. Today, take five minutes to observe the less noticeable things in the morning:

- the sound of baby birds chirping just outside your window

- the wind rustling through the trees

- the smile on a baby's face

Find fascination in something that others might shrug off. Look at the world with new eyes. Take notice of the little things. Life is brimming over with wondrous and spectacular happenings right under your nose. You simply need to open yourself to the precious moments that can provide insight and perspective throughout the rest of your day. ✦

35

dream roll

Dreams can be a window into your subconscious and a source for understanding your deeper self. Follow these simple steps for dream introspection:

① Get a dream journal, or a notebook will do, and keep it just for your morning memories.

② The next time you wake up, roll over in bed and write down what you were dreaming. Don't get up, or you might lose it. Even if you don't normally remember your dreams in the morning, take the time to leave a pen and paper by your bed and simply write down your first thoughts.

③ Don't be concerned with punctuation, grammar, or clarity.

④ Think back on your dream throughout the day.

⑤ See if you start to remember your dreams the more you write them down.

⑥ See if remembering your dreams adds a sense of renewal and meaning in your life.

Often our morning thoughts are like a cloud bank hazing our vision. Give yourself this time to let the fog settle on the horizon and for your mind to come to a clear and rested awareness. ✿

36

a child's eyes

Have you ever noticed how remarkable life is through a child's eyes? Everything is a wonder to be explored. Children often ask a hundred questions about the simplest and most complex things in everyday life. Imagine cultivating some of that wonder and amazement back into your consciousness. Life becomes full of questions, full of excitement and endless fascination.

① Take the next few minutes to fixate on something in your room or just outside your window.

② Pretend you are looking at it through a child's eyes.

③ Take notice of how a child might perceive what you're looking at.

④ Ask yourself very simple questions, like, "What is that?" "How did it get there?" "What is it for?"

When you can recapture your childhood innocence, you remember what is really important in life. You can recall the simple things. You awaken your deeply buried amazement, fascination, bewilderment, and amusement. ✹

37

effortless simplicity

Simplifying a few minor things in your home can make space for inner peace and happiness. Simplicity is the key to achieving lasting harmony. Let's begin with an effortless mental visualization. Start with a picture of your home in your mind. Imagine each room fitting a perfect ideal of a spiritually comforting space. Sunshine is bursting forth from every window. Each room is pleasant, uncluttered, and tidy. Your favorite comfy chair is propped with pillows. Even your plants seem to welcome you when you come in the door. There is a feeling of calmness in every corner. This is your safe haven from a world of chaos. Now make a mental or written wish list for what you could do to achieve this ideal space. Here are some ideas to get you started:

- Fill one bag with clothes and shoes that you haven't worn in years. Give them away.

- Fill a box with books you no longer need.

- Fill a bag of loose magazines and old newspapers for recycling.

- Box up any remaining half-finished projects from six years ago that you're never going to complete.

Clutter in the home brings clutter in your personal life. Clear away some clutter, and you'll be surprised what a relief it can bring. ✺

38

get a new script

We are the stories that we tell. So what if you hate the script? What if you despise your story? You have the power to rewrite your life. You can turn a tragedy into a blessing or a nightmare into a lesson. For example, a woman who had recently gone through an emotionally devastating divorce announced one day that her divorce actually saved her life. Her new story was all about the good fortune that had suddenly come into her life now that she'd been freed to see another side of life. With a few simple lines, you can paint yourself an enviable and rewarding life. Take a few minutes to write an outline for your future.

① Summarize your greatest challenge or hardship at the present moment.

② Take note of the hints of sadness to your story and try flipping it around by rewriting it to sound like your life is really taking a turn for the best.

③ Take a moment to imagine how it would feel to have your life begin to reach its fullest potential and to shed off some of the doom and gloom that can cling to your script.

Tell this new and adventuresome narrative to all your friends and family. ✺

39

listen deeply to another

To be truly present for another is one of life's most precious gifts. How often in conversation are you too busy composing your own response or simply too distracted to hear what another says?

This exercise invites you to practice mindful listening in any early morning conversation.

① Before or during a conversation, breathe mindfully for a few breaths.

② Set your intention. For example, "May I connect more fully by listening mindfully."

③ When the other person speaks, really listen. Look at the person. Hear him or her.

④ Let go of stories in your mind. Don't try to form your reply while the other person is still speaking. Just listen and hear him or her.

⑤ Whenever you feel distracted or bothered in any way, breathe mindfully for a few breaths. And keep listening.

⑥ Be kind and patient with yourself. Attention will wander, and stories will arise in you. Notice and allow these, and return to listening and your breath.

Practice mindful listening to someone else whenever you like. ☀

40

anchor your routine

Most of us can't seem to make the time for ritual. And yet we overlook how rituals are a part of our daily routine—washing the dishes, watering the plants, or folding the laundry. While some of these chores may be loathsome, they can be a source of meditation and inner reflection. Daily habits can anchor your thoughts and feelings just as readily as any spiritual practice or yoga class. This morning, take five minutes to turn a normal, everyday habit into a mindful opportunity for deeper introspection. Consider the following instructions as a guide:

1. Select an activity or chore that you can commit to for five minutes, such as emptying the dishwasher.

2. Clear your mind of all cluttered thoughts and worries.

3. Focus on the movements of your body to achieve this task.

4. Be mindful of your breathing.

5. Take notice of the natural rhythm of your hands, arms, legs, and torso. There is almost a dance to something that you do so instinctively.

6. Take a moment to fully experience the satisfaction of completing the task. Imagine a lightness of being because you now have one less thing to do today.

41

do it now!

There must be a million things you would like to do before you die, before your body gives out, or before this moment passes. You may have said to yourself a thousand times, "I wish I could travel to the Caribbean", "I wish I could finish that art project that I started years ago", "I wish I had a massage appointment once a month." Life is too short to waste another minute. Seize this moment to not procrastinate a single minute more.

The following exercise will help motivate you to not let life's rewards pass you by.

① Take the next few minutes to make a mental or written list of your top five wish-I-could-do-that things. Some of your wishes might be far-fetched; others might be attainable.

② Think about what has been holding you back from reaching attainable goals.

③ Imagine a swift blast of inspirational wind in your sails and select one item that you can start to put near the top of your to-do list.

④ Start scheming to bring your dream within reach. Take baby steps to do what you need to achieve your goal. ✺

42

connect to the natural world

The beauty of nature can offer a sense of peace and vitality that is refreshing and healing. This practice invites you to use mindfulness and the power of each of your senses to connect deeply with the healing power of the natural world. You can do this outside or inside, looking at plants or flowers or water elements.

① Breathe mindfully for about a minute.

②　Set your intention. For example, "May this practice bring me peace and strengthen my connection to nature."

③　After a few more mindful breaths, open your eyes and look at any expression of nature before you. Look mindfully, without judgment and with acceptance. Really see what is there, just as it is. When thoughts come, patiently let them go. Look again, more closely, at shape, color, space, movement, light, and shadow.

④　Close your eyes and shift attention to another sense. Practice mindful hearing, smelling, feeling sensations, even tasting. Attend to and receive deeply what is happening in nature around you, with interest and friendliness, and without judgment.

⑤　End by opening your eyes and moving gently. ☼

relating to yourself
& others

43

find joy in another's good fortune

Does another's good fortune (a vacation, promotion, engagement) ever make you feel jealous or envious, or somehow lessened? Have you noticed how these negative feelings seem to leave you more irritable, isolated, and lonely?

This practice, *sympathetic joy,* is a powerful way to turn away from feelings of insecurity and separation and toward the inherent joy and connection possible in each situation.

① Breathe mindfully for about a minute.

② Set your intention. For example, "May this practice support my relationship with others and diminish feelings of envy and doubt in myself."

③ Sit quietly and think of someone you know who has enjoyed good fortune recently.

④ For the next few minutes, imagine speaking to this person, sensing his or her joy, and saying something like, "May your good fortune never end," or, "May you always be happy."

⑤ Whenever other thoughts or feelings arise in you, kindly let them go and return to the phrases you have selected.

⑥ End by opening your eyes and moving gently. ✵

44

someone who loves you

As humans, we hunger for physical love—a warm embrace, a caring caress, or a sympathetic squeeze of our hand from an old friend. There are many ways to be loving with yourself, to give yourself the tenderness and attention that you need. Take the next five minutes to physically love yourself. Consider the following options:

- Massage your hands, feet, and legs with lotion.

- Give yourself a hug.

- Pick a small bouquet of flowers and put them at your bedside.

- With your eyes closed, gently run your fingers up and down your arms, neck, chest, and stomach.

The time that you put aside for being physically loving and gentle with yourself can have a healing effect on you. Simple pleasures and stimulation can give you a sense of love and compassion in your heart. ☀

45

take a fresh look at yourself

Because of an inner habit of self-criticism and judgment, we rarely sees ourselves accurately, as we are.

This practice invites you to try out a radically different approach to your relationship with yourself. Look deeply and mindfully at yourself, being friendly, nonjudging, and with gratitude.

① Breathe mindfully for about a minute.

②   Set your intention. For example, "May this practice of self-awareness bring me acceptance and wisdom."

③   Breathe mindfully for a few more breaths with your eyes closed.

④   Open your eyes and look at yourself in a mirror. Just look without judgment or self-talk. Acknowledge your physical form completely. Reflect how your body supports you in this life.

⑤   Look more deeply. With kindness and compassion, notice your emotional life—fears, hopes, dreams—without judgment.

⑥   Look again. Acknowledge a source of inspiration, wonder, beauty, mystery, or surprise within you—with gratitude.

⑦   End by breathing deeply once or twice and moving gently. ✿

46

the pulse of life

Nobel peace laureate Bishop Desmond Tutu imparted in his writing an ancient African term to our Western culture, "ubuntu," which encompasses the concept of who we are within the global community. Ubuntu is the essence of all humanity. Western culture thinks almost exclusively in terms of "I" at the unfortunate loss of "we." You can learn to expand your notions of "I" to include "we." Take the next five minutes to see yourself in the greater web of life, intertwined with each and every person, plant, and species on earth. Your existence is inextricably interwoven with their existence. When we can step out of our individualized and compartmentalized lives, we free ourselves to see the bigger picture, to feel more connected with the intoxicating pulse of life and all its wonder. To belong in the greater goodness of all life can bring perspective and compassion into your spirit on a daily basis.

47

lavishing love

"What comes around goes around," an old adage reminds us. To receive love, you must first learn to give love. Making others feel good has a magical way of making you feel good. Take five minutes this morning making a list to lavish a loved one in glorious compliments. Start by putting his or her name at the top of your page. Consider the following endearments to help you get started:

- "You have the nicest smile. It lights up the whole room."

- "You are one of the most generous people I know."

- "You have a way of making everyone feel so loved and cherished in your life."

- "You have the most positive outlook on life, and I really enjoy being around you."

- "Your friendship means the world to me."

- "Thank you for being a part of what is good in my life."

You can either send your list of compliments to your loved one or keep it. A simple act of kindness can be an antidote to selfish gloom. ❁

48

get unglued

Everyone has experienced feeling trapped—stuck in a job you hate, trapped in an unhealthy relationship, or confined to a lifestyle that has you up to your ears in unwanted debt. These are times when you almost feel like you've been permanently glued to something that you can't escape. Take the next five minutes to work on getting unstuck from these pressures. Even if there are no simple solutions to your immediate situation, imagine that there are alternatives just around the corner if you are patient and open to receiving them. Contemplate the prospect that you may be happy under a different arrangement. Ask yourself the following questions to get a sense of choices and options:

- "Why do I feel stuck or trapped?"

- "Do I really need these things in order to be happy?"

- "Could I find fulfillment in other ways, given the opportunity?"

- "What small changes could I make now that might slowly give me the space that I need to find more contentment in my life?" ✸

48

treat yourself as a good friend

If someone asked you to sit down and to write a list of all of your friends—even if you wrote all day—would you think to include yourself? Beginning to think of yourself as a friend is a profound change in self-relationship and a huge step toward healing and wholeness.

In this meditation, you are invited to practice extending kindness to yourself.

① Breathe mindfully for about a minute.

② Set your intention. For example, "May this practice of kindness toward myself nurture ease and self-acceptance."

③ Relax and rest quietly, attending to the breath sensations.

④ Connect with an inner feeling of friendliness by recalling a good friend, a loved one, or a beloved pet.

⑤ For the next few minutes speak to yourself, softly and kindly, repeating a phrase like, "May I be happy, healthy, peaceful, and safe." You could use only one of the words or a different word. Speak to yourself as if you were speaking to a dear friend.

⑥ End by opening your eyes and moving gently. ☀

50

a dose of admiration

While you're still lying in bed, take five minutes to acknowledge the people who have been most influential or inspiring in your life. Take this time to acknowledge that you have a blessed life. Life is a gift. People have been generous and changed your life. Consider the following questions:

- Whom do you admire?

- What qualities do you admire in them?

- What was the best advice that you ever received from them?

- How could you embody the qualities that you admire the most in others?

Sit with these answers and acknowledge what feelings surface for you. Take the time to nurture these endearing qualities in yourself throughout the day. ❁

51

touch and go

Take five minutes in the morning to work out your aches and pains. Do your feet hurt? Or your neck? Pull out some lotion and take the time to massage a tender part of your body.

① Massage your much neglected toes, arches, ankles, and heels.

② Imagine that every spot on the soles of your feet corresponds to an adjacent organ or muscle. For example, when you rub your big toe, you are releasing all the negative thoughts in your brain. When you rub your arches, you are letting go of all the heartache and loss that has built up over the last few months.

③ Do the same with your hands. When you rub your palms, imagine that your sore back is loosening up and relaxing.

④ Work out all the kinks you have from your past and start this day off fresh without them!

Self-massage is about being kind to your body and tending to your emotional injuries too. ✺

52

appreciate yourself

All too often we focus upon what is wrong instead of what is right about ourselves. The consequences of such imbalance include enormous pain and fear.

This practice invites you to restore some balance through mindful attention and appreciation.

① Breathe mindfully for about a minute.

② Set your intention. For example, "May this practice of appreciation quiet self-judgment and criticism in me."

③ Breathe mindfully for a few more breaths, then bring attention to a part of your body. Reflect how it functions and supports your life. For example, lungs support breathing, feet transport you, eyes enable seeing.

④ As you focus, offer your body part a gentle thank you. Now, move on to another part.

⑤ Extend this practice to a quality about yourself, such as loyalty, courage, intelligence, or generosity. Thank that part, also.

⑥ Continue to work with reflection, thanking yourself for your body and inner qualities for a few more minutes.

⑦ End by opening your eyes and moving gently. ✺

53

block walk

We spend a great deal of time indoors, at work, in a car, at the market, at the Laundromat. This morning, take five minutes to walk around the block. Get out of the house and check out your neighborhood.

- Notice how your body feels. Are you tired, sore, rested, or hungry? Pay attention to your body's sensations.

- Notice your surroundings. Is it clear or cloudy? Are there any birds out? Is it windy or calm? Are there gardens around that catch your eye? Are there flowers in bloom that you have never seen before? What do you like or dislike about your neighborhood? What smells attract you? Offer a smile to someone who passes by.

- Take in the sights, sounds, and harmony of life outside your home. Pay attention to details. What do you notice now that you've never noticed before? ☀

54

ritual for release

Acknowledge where there is tension in your body or your mind. Now take five minutes for the following exercise where you envision the release of all tension throughout your mind, body, and soul.

① Stand with your legs shoulder-width apart and solidly planted on the ground. Your arms should be loose at your sides, and your body should feel relaxed but balanced and strong.

② Now lean forward from your hips and let your upper body hang down toward the ground, with your arms loose and fingertips dangling toward the floor.

③ Breathe deeply and relax your body incrementally so that your fingers come closer and closer to the floor and your hips soften and release your torso.

④ Close your eyes and visualize your body being completely relaxed.

⑤ To come up without straining your back, remember to roll up slowly, one vertebra at a time, your head coming up last. Stand upright, relaxed, with your hands at your side.

This is a good exercise for releasing tension. ✺

55

dance your troubles away

Sometimes you simply need permission to go a little mad, or act a little out of character, or to hop around like a clown. When was the last time you danced? This morning, take five minutes to dance around your room to your favorite dance music.

- Put on some screaming James Brown, or the Beatles, or kick up your heels to some country music. Pick out something you know that you simply can't sit still to.

- Lift your arms over your head. Shake your butt like no one is watching. Do the cancan because you can.

Dancing invigorates the body, jump-starts the heart, warms up your muscles, forces you to laugh at yourself, and makes you feel silly. Let's face it, you simply can't feel bad when you're frolicking and skipping around the house to the best guitar solo you've ever heard. ✳

56

gotta love it

Our critical inner voice has a tendency to overshadow our good attributes. But each of us is born into a body that propels us to do fantastic things. We simply need a few minutes to give ourselves some long overdue compliments. Take the next few minutes to stand in front of a mirror and say out loud to yourself at least five things that you like about your body.

- Start at the top of your head and work your way down to your toes.

144

- Think about the compliments that others have given you and include them as well.

- You might list your hair, your nose, your hands, your shapely thighs, your slender back, or your curvy hips.

Your friends might have complimented you on your smile, your sense of style, or your strong legs. Remember these compliments as you carry on with your day. When you feel good about your external self, you will bring confidence and self-esteem into your every step. ☀

57

move it!

Everyone knows the benefits of exercise, but who has time for the gym? Physical movement, however brief, warms up the body, awakens the mind, and enhances flexibility. Take five minutes—use a timer if you need to—to try one of the following movements:

- Run in place in your room.

- Walk briskly around the block.

- Pick up some free weights and work out a routine.

- Lie down and do five minutes worth of sit-ups, leg lifts, and/or push-ups.

When you add a little exercise to your morning routine, you can connect with your body more deeply and release tension. ☀

58

tip the scales

Take a moment to weigh the good with the bad. For some of us, the bad might outweigh the good. This is an opportunity to swing the positive scales in your favor. Take a few minutes and make a mental or written list of every positive thing you can think of to tip the scales to the positive side. To help you get started, complete the following lines:

- "I'm really good at _____ [for example, working, painting, writing]."

- "I have many things in my life that give me pleasure and meaning, like _____ [friends and family, hobbies, gardening]."

- "I've made it this far because I'm _____ [strong, resilient, patient]."

- "Because of my experience, I am more _____ [compassionate, understanding, generous]."

A mental scale comes in handy when you start to feel as if all you can focus on is the negative. With a little effort, you beat the avalanche of bad days by carrying around a reminder list of what is good and constant in your life. ✺

59

comfort yourself

How do you treat your own pain? Whether pain is physical, emotional, or situational, too often our inner response is to be angry, judgmental, and rejecting.

This meditation invites you to approach any pain in yourself with compassion and kindness, instead of anger and rejection.

① Breathe mindfully for about a minute.

② Set your intention. For example, "May this practice strengthen my ability to face suffering in myself and others."

③ Breathe mindfully for a few more breaths.

④ Now, reflect upon a condition or situation in your life that causes you pain.

⑤ Focus upon the pain in yourself around this situation. Allow it. Acknowledge your own pain.

⑥ Speak kindly to yourself, as a parent would to an injured child. Say something like, "May I be at peace. May I be at ease. May I be free from pain."

⑦ End by opening your eyes and moving gently. ☀

60

release the trap

When stressful thoughts inundate us, we all need a quick-fix coping technique. Coping mantras are a simple way to redirect your focus away from anxious thoughts. Positive coping statements enable you to talk yourself through any stressful occurrence. Here are some possible affirmations that will help guide you in your efforts to remain calm and focused. Speak these words aloud:

- "My anxiety will soon pass."

- "I am okay. I am safe. I can cope with any stress that comes my way."

- "I have support and love from others around me."

- "I trust my ability to handle this stress in a calm way."

- "I am choosing to relax now because there will be time later to take action."

Carry these strengthening and calming coping declarations with you throughout your day. By giving yourself permission to find your calm, centered place, you move away from the trapped feelings of anxiety and put yourself in a more pleasant frame of mind. ✸

61

steps to change

We often confuse change with giant leaps forward and overnight results. The reality is that we need to take simple and gradual steps to make lasting change in our lives. Take a few minutes to think about one thing about yourself that you want to change over time and begin to imagine what those baby steps would look like for you.

Ask yourself the following questions to help guide you to achieving your ultimate goal:

- What is your goal? State it clearly and make sure it's reasonable.

- What is your plan of action?

- What are you doing now that can help you reach your goal?

Outlining the steps you need to achieve your goals facilitates your ability to focus. Goal-oriented tasks, however small, give you direction and purpose in life. ✵

look deeply at another

Feelings of separation and loneliness can be strong. It is easy to ignore others, and to live in an inner world feeling isolated and different.

This practice invites you to explore connection with another in a way that feels safe for you.

①   Breathe mindfully for about a minute.

②   Set your intention. For example, "May this practice strengthen my relationships with others."

③   Select a photograph or other image of a loved one.

④   Breathe mindfully for a few breaths. Now focus all of your attention on the image.

⑤   See the person as if for the first time. Drop all the old stories about him or her. Notice as many details as you can.

⑥   Imagine this person moving through the stages of life, as a child, adolescent, adult, in old age, and at death.

⑦   See in this person the same wishes and fears everyone has. See the desire for love, safety, and peace.

⑧   End by releasing the image and noticing your own thoughts and feelings without judgment. ☀

63

the balancing act

Life is a delicate balancing act between what we have to do and what we would like to be doing if we had it our way. Optimal balance between our must-do items and what gives us pleasure requires a well-thought-out game plan. It requires examining your major life commitments and visualizing how they complete a picture of where you are now. For the next few minutes, sit and think about your priorities. Make a mental or written list of the most important things in your life. Your list might include work, child care, errands, and more work. What's missing? Now make a separate list of what you may be neglecting or wish you had more time for. This list might include the following:

- exercise

- playtime

- cooking

- time for family and friends

- movies

- personal hobbies

- afternoon power naps.

Find ways to incorporate more of the things you love to do into your must-do list. Finding balance in your life will instill more harmony and contentment throughout your routine. ❀

64

say thank you

This practice is simple, yet profound—and possibly difficult. It invites you to explore and to experience more fully the power of gratitude.

① Sitting comfortably either indoors or outdoors, breathe mindfully for about a minute.

② Set your intention. For example, "May this practice give me peace and joy."

③ Close your eyes and breathe mindfully for a few more breaths.

④ Open your eyes and look around. As your gaze falls on each thing, silently say thank you (even if it seems to make no sense!). For example, to a plant—thank you. To a chair—thank you. To a tree—thank you. To a computer—thank you.

⑤ As you do this, gently let go of any additional thoughts or stories that your mind creates about the objects. Just do the practice: say thank you.

⑥ Continue for a few more minutes, noticing your own thoughts and feelings without judgment.

⑦ End with a few mindful breaths. ✺

65

drop the past

Past memories of loss can cling to us like old scars that never fade. The more we think about them, the more they feed our sense of failure, pain, and fears. Living in regret is an unhealthy place to dwell for any length of time. Try this easy exercise for a few minutes this morning.

① Make a mental or written list of your top two worst memories: for example, death of your parents, an unhappy five-year marriage.

② Think about how you felt about each bad experience: "Death terrifies me," or, "I'll never love anyone again."

③ Put a positive spin on each lesson that you learned: "Death is part of life," or, "The first two years of marriage were good."

④ Remember the following affirmation to help you stay in a positive frame of mind: "I have come this far, and I am stronger for it."

When you can find the inner strength that helped you through the difficult times in your past, you can more readily drop the self-defeating thoughts that plague your momentum forward to a more hopeful peace of mind. ❀

66

you come first

Many of us go through life as people pleasers, giving and helping others without taking much time to figure out what we really need to be happy. To recognize what you need, you have to put yourself first. You have to give yourself permission to think for yourself and listen carefully to your inner voice that knows exactly what you need and how to meet that need. It means the next time you catch yourself declining your needs for someone else—such as making plans with someone you really don't want to spend time with—try to stop yourself for just a moment and say, "This isn't what I want and that's okay. I need to do what's best for me."

When in doubt about what you need, you may have a tendency to ask others what they think you should do. Instead, ask yourself the following questions:

- "How do I reconnect with my true inner desires, wants, and needs?"

- "How can I keep the voice of 'woulda-shoulda-coulda' out of my head?"

- "How can I first make my needs important and valued, instead of always putting other's needs first?"

It will take some practice, but over time you will gain the skills to put yourself first. ✺

67

appreciate a loved one

We are constantly receiving blessings and the benefits of love and support from others. Yet how often do we stop to acknowledge them?

This practice invites deeper appreciation for the gifts of others and what they add to your inner and outer life.

① Breathe mindfully for about a minute.

② Set your intention. For example, "May this practice deepen my connection with _____ [say your loved one's name here]."

③ Breathe mindfully for a few breaths. Now picture the loved one you wish to appreciate.

④ Reflect on his or her positive presence in your life. Whisper a quiet thank you.

⑤ Reflect on how this person has supported you. Say thank you.

⑥ Reflect on how this person has loved you. Say thank you.

⑦ End by breathing mindfully for a few breaths.

The next time you speak with your loved one, thank him or her. ✳

68

jet fuel in the morning

Breakfast is the most important meal of the day. It's your jet fuel to get your day started and to keep your energy up to par. So before you skip breakfast again or wolf down some empty carbohydrates in a mad dash for work, take a few moments to respect what you put into your body. When you make time for a healthy, sit-down meal in the morning, you allow your body to properly digest, relax, and reduce stress. This morning, before you eat breakfast, slow down for five minutes. Here are some ways to eat mindfully.

- Pick out something delicious and nutritious for your breakfast, such as a piece of fruit, yogurt, or almond butter on toast.

- Clear away space at the table to be present with your meal. Remove interruptions. Turn off the news. Put away your book.

- Take a good, long look at your food. Take in the smell, the taste, and the various colors.

- Take notice of your hunger, your mouth, your belly, and the sensations in your body.

- Imagine that each bite of food is filling your whole being with energy. Picture every mineral and vitamin being absorbed into your body. ❀

69

be your own best friend

It is scary for many of us to face being alone. We fill our calendars with endless social dates in order to avoid the simple act of spending time on our own. Being with yourself is essential to finding inner joy. Take the next few minutes to imagine what you could do alone for fun that you would normally do with others.

- Make a dinner date out for yourself.

- Find a place to go hiking by yourself.

- Take yourself out to a movie.

- Head over to the gym for a workout or swim.

To be your own best friend requires trying things that you may not be accustomed to. But there are rewards. When you strengthen your ability to nurture yourself without any help from others, you reconnect with who you are and what you love. ❁

70

notice the world around you

Do you ever miss what is happening right in front of you because your attention is somewhere else?

This practice can be used anywhere. It can be done at home or elsewhere, as part of the opening activity in your daily schedule. It invites you to connect mindfully with life as it is happening.

① Wherever you are—at home, at work, in nature— stop and breathe mindfully for about a minute.

② Set your intention. For example, "May this practice help me connect with my life more deeply."

③ Breathe mindfully for a few more breaths and begin to look around.

④ Pour your wholehearted attention into the experience. Notice sights, sounds, smells, tastes, and sensations as they happen, without trying to add or subtract anything.

⑤ Whenever thoughts or judgments arise, gently let them go, and return your attention to the experience of each of your senses.

⑥ Rest in a spirit of discovery. Marvel at what you can notice in your world. Enjoy being surprised.

You can continue as long as you wish. Practice as often as you wish, anywhere, anytime. ✳

growing wiser
& kinder

71

name the pain

Upset in mind and body often continues because we have not given it enough compassionate attention. There is great power in turning kind observation and attention toward any inner unpleasantness.

This practice invites you to welcome demanding inner visitors with acceptance and attention by naming and watching them.

① Breathe mindfully for about a minute.

②   Set your intention. For example, "May this practice of naming and acceptance give me ease and energy."

③   Breath mindfully for a few breaths.

④   Notice any aspect of your experience beyond your breath that demands attention. For example, worried thoughts, intense feelings of sadness or fear, or unpleasant sensations or sounds.

⑤   Softly and patiently name the demanding experience. Do not try to change it or make it go away. Just repeatedly name it—worry, fear, thinking— holding it in focus and observing it. Allow it to be just as it is. You may have to name it many times.

⑥   Notice how the experience changes and how other experiences flow in and out of the present moment.

⑦   End by opening your eyes and moving gently. ☀

72

give grace

Spirituality can be as simple as incorporating small rituals into your daily routine. Regardless of what religion you practice, giving grace or being mindful for all the bounty in your life is a rewarding experience. You can do this at breakfast. If you're in a rush, at least stop and sit for five minutes before you run out the door with your toasted bagel in hand. Close your eyes, inhale deeply and exhale three times, and say aloud a few things that you are thankful for. You might consider saying the following:

- "I am grateful for this food on my plate."

- "I am grateful for the unexpected joy that this day might bring."

- "I am thankful for this spoon, cup, napkin, and plate."

- "I appreciate this moment to be able to sit with my meal and enjoy every bite."

- "I am blessed by this nourishing food and beverage, and I know it will give me energy throughout my day."

73

just when you thought
you were alone

Everyone has experienced agonizing loneliness at some point in their life. Whether you're single or married, have children or live alone, no one is exempt from feelings of isolation. This is an exercise in global consciousness. There are people all over the planet who feel the same yearning and suffering to be connected.

① Take a moment to reflect on a time when you felt desperately alone.

② Now imagine creating a circle of support in your own bedroom.

③ A close friend walks in, sits down beside you, squeezes your shoulder gently, and reassures you that he or she knows exactly what you're feeling.

④ Several more people appear like a support group to remind you that you are not alone. They have felt this lonely and isolated at times, but now you are in it together.

Remember your visual support group for those times when you feel most abandoned. By creating your own visual support, you are taking the steps to heal the wound of loneliness and finding creative ways to bring forth compassion into your daily routine. ✺

74

gorgeous on the inside

When we're not being too critical of our physical attributes, we often get caught up in being too critical of our personal characteristics, or who we are on the inside. How often have you heard yourself say, "I'm dumb", "I'm not artistic", "I was never good at that?" Take a few minutes to stand in front of a mirror and say aloud no less than five personality traits that you like about yourself. Consider the compliments that you've received from others and include them in your list. Your strengths might consist of your ability to be loving, kind to others, nurturing, generous, open to new ideas and people, or funny. Your friends may have told you that you are a great conversationalist, fun to be around, caring, sensitive, or a good listener. The positive way you feel about yourself on the inside has a remarkable way of shining through to the person you are on the outside.

75

begin to heal your own deep pain

Compassionate attention and presence have remarkable healing powers. Learning to stay present for intense pain is a powerful gift for healing and transformation. By cultivating your capacity for offering accepting attention in challenging situations, you can assist healing in yourself and in others.

This practice aims at strengthening your capacity to stay present and open to pain in yourself.

① Breathe mindfully for about a minute.

② Set your intention. For example, "May this practice empower me to remain present and to heal pain in myself and in others."

③ Breathe mindfully for a few more breaths.

④ Now, deliberately think of a painful or challenging situation in your life.

⑤ Notice and allow all feelings and thoughts that arise around this situation.

⑥ As you breathe in, name and acknowledge any pain, feelings, or thoughts connected to this situation.

⑦ As you breathe out, speak to each one saying something like, "May you be at peace."

⑧ End by opening your eyes and moving gently. ☀

76

a shot of faith

Faith is a concept that means different things to different people. Used here, faith simply means the understanding that life is a mystery, and living in the mystery is what life is all about. Life is full of "what ifs" and "whys." Each of us has inner core beliefs about life, love, and the principles that guide us in how we live. For the next five minutes, take an imaginary journey to connect with your inner, personal faith. Start this visualization with three deep breaths. Imagine that you have come to the edge of all that you know and are about to step off into the dark of the unknown.

① Think of a challenge you are facing in your life at this time.

② What are your thoughts, fears, or concerns?

③ Now visualize that same challenge working out perfectly.

④ Notice how different it feels to let go and to have faith that you have everything it takes in life to face that challenge.

Believing in yourself gives you strength and resiliency.

77

bold, fearless, and powerful

True acts of bravery are much easier to notice in others than in yourself. Each of us, though, has at least done one or two things in life that proved to be real acts of courage. A woman who has given birth is very brave. It takes bravery to find the strength to ask for help when you really need it. It takes a courageous person to quit his or her job and find a better one. Take the next five minutes to recall the times in your life, however brief or small, when you faced something challenging and found the power to overcome it.

① Think of a time that you acted bravely.

② What was hard about it?

③ How did it feel to be brave?

④ What can you do to commit to an act of bravery today?

The times that you have triumphed over adversity are living proof that you are a person who is capable of being bold, fearless, and powerful. ✹

78

face death with wisdom
and compassion

How you live and what you believe can have a profound impact on how you face life, the process of dying, and the moment of death.

This practice invites you to use compassionate imagination to explore your own ideas about death. You may change how you live as a result.

① Breathe mindfully for about a minute.

② Set your intention. For example, "May this practice help me to enrich my life and to face death."

③ Take a minute or two and, using two or three sentences or key words like "hospital," "alone," or "afraid," describe how you imagine your death will be. Be specific and concrete and as detailed as you can. Describe the what, when, who, and where.

④ When you are done, pause and take a few mindful breaths.

⑤ Now, take a minute or two and describe how you would *like* your death to be, in the same detail, using two to three sentences or a few key words.

⑥ Review your descriptions. Reflect on them. Can you live your life in a way that supports the description you would prefer? What would that mean? Where and how could you begin to live that way? ☀

79

mine your power

There are times in our lives when we feel powerless to change. We feel ineffectual and unable to tap into our strengths. This exercise is about imagining that you are a miner excavating the golden nuggets in your personality. Find the gold that turns a powerless situation into an empowering one. Take the next five minutes to contemplate or write down the following:

① Consider the tools and skills that you already have in your tool bag. What are you good at?

② List five strengths.

③ Think about the things that people have complimented you for.

④ Remember a time when you were able to overcome a
particularly difficult situation.

Create opportunities to let these positive qualities shine
through your personality every day. ✺

80

open the door to wisdom

None of us feels great when we make a mistake. However small, it can aggravate us to no end. But mistakes can also be gifts, doorways to learning, growth, and wisdom. When you open your mind to what mistakes can represent, you can stop punishing yourself and learn to grow. For the next few minutes, think of the last mistake you made. Then consider the following questions:

- What about the mistake was disappointing, frustrating, or aggravating?

- What lesson did you take away from the mistake?

- How can you put a more positive twist on your mistake to frame it in a more empowering way?

The greatest lessons in life often originate from a place of failure. Mistakes can be excellent teachers who guide you along a bumpy road to a place of understanding. The next time you make an error, give yourself permission to be open to the valuable lesson that will improve your life. ☀

81

feel your connection with all things

Using phrases linked to the process of inhaling and exhaling, this practice offers the opportunity to explore your connections in the web of life.

① Breathe mindfully for about a minute.

② Set your intention. For example, "May this practice open my heart more deeply."

③ Focus attention on your breath.

④ Link silent phrases with each in-breath and out-breath as follows:

- "Breathing in, I feel breath supporting my life."
- "Breathing out, I say thank you for being alive."
- "Breathing in, I know all living things must breathe."
- "Breathing out, I feel my connection with all living things."
- "Breathing in, I wish happiness and peace for myself."
- "Breathing out, I see that all living things wish happiness and peace."

⑤ Explore linking breath to any other phrases that appeal to you.

⑥ End by opening your eyes and moving gently. ☀

82

honor your commitments

Take a few minutes to make a mental or written list of five commitments that you would like to make to yourself and for yourself today. Here are some examples to help you get started:

- "I am committed to doing the best I can today, and my best is good enough."

- "I am committed to giving and receiving more love every day."

- "I am committed to addressing my health issues and learning new ways to promote my well-being."

- "I am committed to making new friends."

- "I am committed to making time in my schedule for an exercise program."

Commitments are challenging but rewarding. When you make the effort to list your goals, you activate your potential for achievement. Setting goals gives you direction, focus, and intention in your life. ❁

83

the highway of life

The highway of life doesn't come with a convenient road map. We all stumble along trying to make sense of our daily unfoldings. However, each of us has an imaginary, inner guide that can help steer and direct us. Your personal guide is your connection to your insight and intuition. Your guide is someone or something that can escort you to a safe place. Follow these steps to find your guide.

① Imagine for a moment that your inner guide is a caring and loving person in your life. Visualize him or her standing beside you.

② Ask your special guide to help you find support and a place of calm. Invite your guide to lead you to a path of relaxation.

③ Let your inner guide take your hand and show you the way. Notice how it feels to have your guide by your side.

④ Listen to the words your guide says to you. Watch your guide's pace.

⑤ Once you arrive at your calm place, practice saying the following affirmation: "This is a good place to relax. I am free to let go of my tension here."

With practice, this exercise will empty your mind of tension and open you to unexpected answers. ✺

84

be a mountain

This is a good practice for those times when you are feeling scattered, off balance, or unfocused.

It allows you to reconnect with the elemental quality of earthiness and strength within. Doing this practice can ground you deeply in the present moment.

① Stand or sit comfortably.

② Breathe mindfully for about a minute.

③ Set your intention. For example, "May this practice help me find inner strength."

④ Imagine the most beautiful mountain you have ever seen, either in person or in a photograph.

⑤ As you visualize your mountain, let your body become the mountain. Feel the same qualities of steadiness, strength, unshakableness, and majesty.

⑥ For the next few minutes, rest in your "mountain body," unmoved by any thoughts, fears, worries, or other experiences around you, just as the mountain is unmoved by any weather patterns around it.

⑦ End by opening your eyes and moving gently. ✺

85

one-way ticket to the moon

Each of us carries around some emotional burdens that we would like to discard. Wouldn't it be great if you could simply pack up all of your emotional baggage, purchase a one-way ticket to send the suitcase to the moon, and then throw a good-riddance party? Forgive yourself today. Take the next few minutes to complete the following forgiveness exercises. Fill in the blanks.

- "Today is a good day to forgive myself for
  _____."

- "I can be hard on myself when I _____, so today I am letting it go."

- "I'm still mad at myself for _____, but today I am forgiving and forgetting."

- "For all those years that I held on to the pain of _____, today I am freeing myself to feel exonerated."

Give yourself a free ticket to forgiveness. Let go of the weight of your troubles and ease your mind. ✺

86

cultivate gratitude

Headlines scream, "200 Killed in Plane Crash." They rarely say, "15,000 Planes Landed Safely Yesterday." The tendency to focus on the negative can become a habit that separates us in fear and obscures the richness of life.

This practice invites you to turn toward the good in your life and to express gratitude as recognition grows.

① Breathe mindfully for about a minute.

② Set your intention. For example, "May this practice open my eyes in wonder and appreciation."

③ Breathe mindfully for a few more breaths.

④ Now reflect on something in your life that works or supports you. For example, "My heart is strong," or, "My father is well," or, "My e-mail got through." Quietly say thank you.

⑤ Reflect on something that—in its absence—is good. For example, *no* toothache, or *no* sickness in a loved one, or *no* hurricane or tornado. Quietly say thank you.

⑥ End by opening your eyes and moving gently.

87

fuel your optimism

Our pessimism can sometimes get the better of us. How many times have you told yourself, "It won't work. Nothing good ever happens to me." Start your morning with a five-minute prayer for hope. List as many hopeful thoughts for yourself, your loved ones, the planet, and the universe as you can think of. Here are some hope-filled suggestions to get you started:

- "I have hope today that everything will go smoothly at work."

- "I have hope today that my family is healthy and happy."

- "I have hope today that my pet is feeling safe and content."

- "I have hope today that my friends and loved ones are having good experiences in life."

- "I have hope today that peace on earth will infect the planet and restore harmony."

Hope breeds positive thinking. Optimism will fuel the whole day ahead of you. ✺

88

the doctor is in

Each of us has the ability to be a healer. It is an ancient wisdom and gift deeply ingrained in our species, but rarely do we give ourselves the permission to cultivate our healing nature. Take a few minutes and scan your mind and body for areas of pain or discomfort whether physical or emotional. Become your own shaman. Ask your higher self what you need to help assist you in healing your aches and pains.

- Do you need more rest?

- Do you need more water?

- How does your body feel and what can you do for yourself to feel better?

- Would a cup of herbal tea help you to relax right now?

Cultivate your inner healer and imagine that you have the insight and power to meet all of your health needs. ✺

89

where the soul lives

There are times when we need to turn inward toward our spiritual self in order to seek wisdom and clarity. When we look deeper into this soulful place within ourselves, we come closer to experiencing the rewarding journey of all that life has to offer.

Try to visualize an intangible space within the very core of your being that contains your soul. Imagine a doorway that gives you a direct passageway to open your life, spirit, and higher self to all the beauty, wonder, and mystery of the universe. By opening yourself in a spiritual way, you will see the world afresh and with a new perspective. You may want to say the following positive affirmations aloud:

- "Today, I am opening my soul to love and satisfying connections."

- "Today, I am opening my soul to beauty, truth, and wisdom."

- "Today, I am opening my soul to joy, laughter, and whimsy."

- "Today, I am opening my soul to _____." (Fill in the blank.)

Opening a doorway to your soul is a way of bringing more meaning into your life. Meaning gives a sense of purpose and hope to your entire day. ❁

90

live in this moment

Life is happening in this moment, yet how much of your attention is directed to planning for the future or trying to undo or correct the past (even when you don't need or want to be planning or correcting)?

This practice helps you become more aware of the habit of the mind to move out of the present moment. Recognizing habits of inattention and absence will empower you to become free and to live more fully in the present.

①   Breathe mindfully for about a minute.

②   Set your intention. For example, "May this practice free me from habits of absence and inattention."

③   For the next few minutes, notice any thoughts you have directed at either the future or the past. Acknowledge them and say thank you. You don't have to fight with them. Just let them go.

④   If you become distracted or confused, breathe mindfully for a few breaths. When you are focused again, return your attention to the thoughts. Learn to recognize when your attention goes to the future or to the past.

⑤   End by opening your eyes and moving gently.   ✲

91

dig yourself out of the pit

When you're in the dire pit of despair, it is easy to lose perspective on how fortunate you truly are. For the next few minutes, try this simple exercise to enlarge your perspective.

① Begin by broadening the way you view the world. Think of another culture that is very different from your own.

② From this larger cultural context, imagine what real day-to-day poverty must feel like.

③ Imagine if there were unlimited global resources, such that every human could get their basic needs met. This may require visualizing those with more giving up some of their resources for those with less.

④ Add up your blessings and be grateful for what you have.

When you open yourself to what others are struggling with, you may find that your own personal problems seem less burdensome and troubling. ✸

92

spell it out

What's an acronym have to do with your soul? It may appear silly at first glance, but this exercise is based on the premise that positive affirmations, mantras, or even acronyms can feed your soul. One way to do this is to formulate a small mental or written list of some things you want to do or become. Now, take this list of four or five affirmations and create a positive acronym to help you remember the elements of the list. For example, if your acronym is LIFE, your list might include the following:

<u>L</u>aughter

<u>I</u>nner peace

<u>F</u>un with friends

<u>E</u>ating healthy

Write your acronym down and keep it with you as a daily reminder to nurture your soul, enjoy every day, and expand your awareness. ❁

93

retire the judges in your mind

The habit of judging—others, yourself, the world around you—can become a kind of addiction that creates unnecessary feelings of fear and isolation.

This practice offers the promise of more freedom from your judging mind by making you more mindful of the actual process of judgmental thinking.

① Breathe mindfully for about a minute.

② Set your intention. For example, "May this practice free me from the prison of judgmental thinking."

③ Breathe mindfully for a few more breaths.

④ Pay attention to any thoughts you may have, especially judgmental thoughts. For example, "This is good," "This is bad," "I like this," "I don't like that," and so on.

⑤ Notice self-judgments and self-criticism.

⑥ Notice the tone of your judgmental thoughts.

⑦ To all of the judgments, say, "Thank you, you may or may not be true, but thank you anyway." You do not have to fight the judgments or argue with them in any way. Just notice them and let them be.

⑧ End by opening your eyes and moving gently.

94

creative juice squeeze

In your hurried, busy life, you may often neglect time for your creative self to emerge. You may feel like doing art is unnecessary, or you can't be bothered with doing art, or you feel guilty trying to make time for it. Creative outlets are a healthy and important way to nourish your soul. Take the next few minutes this morning to do a creative project to enrich your life.

- Write one sentence of a poem.

- Sing a song to your plants.

- Paint a feeling or a mood with only a few brush strokes.

- Display your breakfast in an artistic way.

What matters is not how much time you invest in the creative activity but that you make a small effort to open your creative core and let the sunshine in. Art intoxicates the mind, tickles the spirit, and colors your life with beauty and creativity. Squeeze the most out of your hidden creative forces today. ✺

95

no more grumpy mornings

Here is an antidote for waking up grumpy. Try writing down all the good things that happened to you over the past week. It's not as easy as you think. But by making a mental list of a couple of sweet moments, you can sweep away your negativity and replace it with gratitude. Here are some suggestions to help trigger your memory:

- A neighbor complimented you on your blouse.

- A friend called to thank you for something you did to help out.

- A stranger insisted that you go ahead of him at a long check-out line at the market.

- You saw a small child trying to take some wobbly steps, and it made you smile inside.

- You noticed that one of your houseplants has just started to blossom.

- Someone smiled at you on the way to work.

The smallest act or the briefest occasion is all it takes to remind you of the beauty in your life. ✳

96

"no" is not a four-letter word

In your efforts to be generous and self-sacrificing, you may forget how to set firm boundaries so that you don't get taken advantage of or taken for granted. You can't please everyone all of the time. Learn how to identify when you are tired and need permission to say, "I'm sorry. I can't do that today." When you set healthy limits on what you can and cannot do, you simplify your life and become more present in the activities that you do take on. Boundaries are important because they shape who you are and what you are capable of giving. Reading the following simple exercise in the morning will help strengthen your boundaries ahead of time.

- The next time you feel yourself buckling under to pressure, stop what you're doing and give yourself permission to defend your boundary. Say no when you need to.

- Be clear in your commitments to others. Minimize doing more than your fair share by stating clearly from the start what you can and cannot do.

- When your boundaries are threatened, speak up and state your boundary again. You may even need to redirect the conversation or physically remove yourself from the situation.

With practice, learning to say no will give you a stronger sense of self-worth and personal freedom. ☀

97

find life in death

Death is unavoidable. And the exact time and circumstances of when you will die are unknown. Rather than fear or attempt to deny these facts, you can use them as a basis for inquiry and as a guide for skillful living.

The following meditative exercise should be done with a spirit of curiosity and with a sense of kindness and compassion for yourself and your life.

① Breathe mindfully for about a minute.

②   Set your intention. For example, "May this practice enable me to feel more peace and to meet life's challenges more wisely and kindly."

③   Continue mindful breathing.

④   When you feel centered, as if tossing a pebble into a still pond, deliberately ask yourself the question, "Knowing that my life will end, what is my deepest value?" Or, "Knowing that my life will end, what is most important to me?"

⑤   Listen respectfully for the answer from within. It may be a word, a phrase, an image, or something else. Repeat your question and listen for as long as you like.

⑥   End by opening your eyes and moving gently. ✺

98

infinite impossibilities

Lewis Carroll, the whimsical, magical author of *Alice in Wonderland,* once wrote of the notion of believing in the impossible. The power of suggestion and belief are fierce antidotes to situations of helplessness. Open your heart and mind to infinite potential and possibilities. Imagine a fantasy world where all of your needs and desires would be satisfied. Take a few minutes to write down what your fantasy world would look, feel, smell, taste, and sound like. Ask yourself the following questions:

- What would your relationship with your partner be like?

- What kind of housing would you live in?

- Where in the world would you live?

- What negative aspects of life would you get rid of?

Now, try to illustrate one of these dreams, even if it's as simple as creating a collage of your dream home. Or try saying something unexpectedly nice to your loved one. Some of the greatest thinkers of our time achieved what they did because they were willing to open their minds to the unimaginable, the inconceivable, and the exquisite vastness beyond perception. Go on . . . give it a try. ✻

99

give yourself praise

You accomplish dozens of things every day. But do you remember to thank yourself? Do you think to reward yourself with some much-needed praise for all the wonderful things you do that often go unnoticed? This morning is your chance to be grateful for all the little things you do to make your life and others' lives simpler and smoother. Make a mental or written list of five things you did yesterday that helped out someone else, and then give yourself a hug or thank yourself out loud. When you take the time to acknowledge all the things you do, you remind yourself that you are a marvelous and magnificent person. Here's what your list might reflect:

- "I am thanking myself for giving up my weekend to clean house."

- "I am thanking myself for going over and beyond my call of duties at work."

- "I am thanking myself for taking such good care of my friends and family."

- "I am thanking myself for being a good friend to others in their times of need."

- "I am thanking myself for taking everyone out for dinner."

You deserve a round of applause and a song of praise every day. ✸

100

open to the mystery of being human

So much of the misery and pain of human life rests upon feelings of fear, separation, and judgment.

This practice invites you to explore some other human possibilities—through meditative reflection, imagination, and inner wisdom.

①   Breathe mindfully for about a minute.

② Set your intention. For example, "May this practice awaken me to more possibility."

③ Breathe mindfully for a few more breaths.

④ Ask yourself the following questions:

- "What would it be like to feel more love in my life?"

- "What if I didn't have to always be right?"

- "What would it feel like to be flowing *with* life, not against it?"

- "What would it be like to love another more generously?"

⑤ After each question, breathe mindfully and listen for whatever answer arises. Work with one question, more than one, or make up your own.

⑥ End by opening your eyes and moving gently. ✺

Jeffrey Brantley, MD, is a consulting associate in the Duke University Department of Psychiatry in Durham, NC. He is founder and director of the Mindfulness-Based Stress Reduction Program at Duke University's Center for Integrative Medicine, as a spokesperson for which he has given many radio, television, and print media interviews. He is the author of *Calming Your Anxious Mind*.

Wendy Millstine is a Bay-Area-based freelance writer, published poet, and performance artist.

Some Other New Harbinger Titles

Talk to Me, Item 3317 $12.95

Romantic Intelligence, Item 3309 $15.95

Transformational Divorce, Item 3414 $13.95

Eating Mindfully, Item 3503 $13.95

Sex Talk, Item 2868 $12.95

Everyday Adventures for the Soul, Item 2981 $11.95

Love Tune-Ups, Item 2744 $10.95

The Deepest Blue, Item 2531 $13.95

The 50 Best Ways to Simplify Your Life, Item 2558 $11.95

Brave New You, Item 2590 $13.95

The Conscious Bride, Item 2132 $12.95

Juicy Tomatoes, Item 2175 $13.95

The Money Mystique, Item 2221 $13.95

Call toll free, **1-800-748-6273,** or log on to our online bookstore at www.newharbinger.com to order. Have your Visa or Mastercard number ready. Or send a check for the titles you want to New Harbinger Publications, Inc., 5674 Shattuck Ave., Oakland, CA 94609. Include $4.50 for the first book and 75¢ for each additional book, to cover shipping and handling. (California residents please include appropriate sales tax.) Allow two to five weeks for delivery.

Prices subject to change without notice.